Rose Cook's poems are often poignant, reflecting the many variables of ordinary lives, but always with a lightness of touch, an acceptance of what it is to be human. A collection fluid and sincere, the poems are wide ranging, sometimes painterly, sometimes with a wonderful down-to-earth diction and a singular inwardness that delights.

Denise McSheehy,
author of *Salt*

In their transparency and deceptive simplicity Rose Cook's poems reveal pure and hidden depths in nature, memory and loss, celebrating and questioning the fragility of everyday interactions. These are indeed poems for people 'who juggle [their] lives', insisting in their gratitude that we 'be still sometimes'. To read *Notes From a Bright Field* is to be renewed in body, mind and spirit.

Anthony Wilson,
author of *Riddance*

To listen to Rose Cook is to be taken into a room that you didn't know existed. There is something to be savoured in every line.

Matt Harvey,
writer, poet, performer and host of Radio 4's
Wondermentalist Cabaret. His latest book is
Mindless Body, Spineless Mind.

She has a unique way with words, variously funny, sad, tender and true. Her writing delights ingeniously in itself and the world at large. The delight is infectious.

Helena Nelson,
editor of Happen*Stance* Press

In *Taking Flight* Rose Cook evokes strong moods in the reader and inspires many imaginative flights. Hers is a poetry of love and in particular of longing, experienced through different times and in different situations and which culminates movingly and compellingly in the second section, The Blank Child. This is a very entertaining and readable collection; for many I suspect it will become a very important one too.

Colin Brown,
director of Poetry Can, Bristol

Rose Cook's hard-won poems do justice to the complexities of ordinary human experience in admirably precise and natural language.

Michael Laskey,
poet, editor, founder of the Aldeburgh Poetry Festival

Rose Cook is a poet whose words fly off the page with great elegance and beauty. These poems are full of love and loss captured with a lightness of touch that makes them a joy to read.

Sarah Ellis,
digital producer for the Royal Shakespeare Company

I really enjoy her poems; they give an intense experience, like standing under a radiant tree, face up, eyes closed, and feeling the leaves drop down on you one by one. I felt echoes of Rumi and Mary Oliver, a Mary Oliver for the South Hams instead of New England.

Miriam Darlington,
author of *Otter Country: In Search of the Wild Otter*

Rose Cook's poetry conveys a real sense of sincerity and serenity and has a magnificent life-affirming quality.

Chris Brooks,
poet, performer and founder of Poetry Island
at The Blue Walnut, Torquay

Rose Cook is one of the South-West's best loved poets, having performed extensively in venues such as the Soho Theatre in London, the Bristol Poetry Festival and Dartington's Ways With Words Literature Festival, as well as a variety of local poetry events. She is an Apples & Snakes poet and has appeared at the North Devon Festival in Barnstaple, Plymouth's Barbican theatre, Exeter Phoenix's Text Festival and a Peterloo Poets event in Cornwall.

Rose co-founded the popular Devon poetry and performance forum One Night Stanza, as well as poetry performance group Dangerous Cardigans. Her work has been broadcast on BBC Radio 3, BBC Radio Devon and local SoundArt radio.

She has run writing workshops with older people and offers poems for reading aloud at the Totnes Memory Cafe.

www.rosecook.wordpress.com

NOTES FROM
A BRIGHT FIELD

For Ian,
fellow poet on the path,
love Rose

Also by Rose Cook

Everyday Festival Happen*Stance* Press (2009)
Taking Flight Oversteps Books (2009)

NOTES FROM A BRIGHT FIELD

ROSE COOK

Cultured Llama Publishing

First published in 2013 by
Cultured Llama Publishing
11 London Road
Teynham, Sittingbourne
ME9 9QW
www.culturedllama.co.uk

A CIP record for this book is available from The British Library

ISBN 978-0-9568921-9-5

Printed in Great Britain by Lightning Source UK Ltd

Jacket design by Mark Holihan
Front cover image by Joe Cook
Front cover design by Will Perrens
Copy editing by Anne-Marie Jordan

Contents

Out beyond ideas of wrongdoing and rightdoing,
there is a field. I'll meet you there.

When the soul lies down in that grass,
the world is too full to talk about.

from Out beyond ideas of wrongdoing and rightdoing
by Mevlana Jelaluddin Rumi

I have seen the sun break through
to illuminate a small field
for a while, and gone my way
and forgotten it. But that was the pearl
of great price, the one field that had
treasure in it. I realize now
that I must give all that I have
to possess it.

from The Bright Field
by R. S. Thomas

for Rubin and Iris

I

The World Offers Itself

Twilight

How to begin my song?
Two geese fly over
creaking love,
but how shall I start?

Blackbird calls up the garden
then darkness comes rattling,
owl swings low over meadow,
hide rabbit, hide.
I will begin.

A Skip and a Hop: a Series of Walks

1

The wood grows kinder as we walk,
then noticing begins: bright leaf,
a cobweb catches light.
The sun this time of year shines slant,
the columned trees drawn straight
with leaf-filled hollows, turn a bend to find
a bush ablaze, illuminated as by an angel.

Bird song, twig-snap, cones tumble through.
Wrapped about by trees, walk on,
step over roots, breathe wooded air,
until the furrowed field, with its spinney full of gold.

2

To walk beside a small girl who is happy,
how she dances: skip, hop, bound.
I wonder when we began not to skip?

There she goes, high step, half-step, skip.

3

A labyrinth is not a puzzle at all,
but a single quiet path, in and out,
it is where one can be found.
No shortcuts, but to enjoy the sacred walk.

Walking forward becomes linked to trust,
return again to the fall of breath.
It is the breath alone that signals hope,
that life is here, continuous.

Remember, the bear man said, *the bears don't like me,*
they trust me is all, so are unafraid.
That spider on your shoulder is nothing personal,
you are another entity, part of the whole.

4
After a long walk, return to find
someone has left a flower on the windscreen,
kindness tucked there.

Along With the Tall Trees

On the wires outside,
a swallow cleans its wing feathers,
Krishna blue in the sun.
When I open the door, I find
a dog lying across the threshold.
She follows me out.
Not liking the heavy heat,
the drone of bees,
I seek shade like a snail.
I am here, that is all.

Perhaps it is because
I am not intrepid, never was,
I must make a cup of tea, becoming
more like my mother every ten days.
It is a wonder this life.

In Lucca, we found a labyrinth,
marked where people had reached up
to trace it. It made me happy
and remains outside the church,
with the months of the year, the seasons.

In the busy market square
where people saunter and cycle
while the sun beats down,
I trace the old paths with my finger
switching over, back, under, round
until mesmerised into the within.
The middle of nowhere, someone said.
Just the middle is fine by me.
Yesterday I read:
I am nobody, born of nobody.
Now I am nowhere too.

The Wagtail Tree

There is a tree at the bottom of our town
which every night fills
with a cloud of wagtails.
We stand in the cold air
and look up at the branches.

A hundred small bodies perch in silence,
all facing the same way.
Festive bulbs are strung around their tree,
uplighting their pale breasts, their long tails.
They look like decorations.

This when my mother lies sleeping
through her last Christmas
and my life has a split screen
with her hollowed face in the corner
and me wrapping presents

with a memory of tree dressing,
her hands clipping a silver wagtail to a branch.
Every evening the birds come back
and every morning
there is life to be embraced.

Landscapes With Trees

She comes in early light,
lies her full length along.
There is nothing else, just this
one body against another.
Outside the wind continues its work,
the river rises, carries seeds
from freshly tilled earth.

I want to write about trees,
their comfort, but only remember
the great yew, from which thin bones fall
to catch in the gullets of dogs.
I want the taste of forest air,
to listen for the in-between silence.

In my last days, I will plant trees, release them
to begin their long reach into ground.
When I am gone, there will be branch and canopy,
with deep shadow below. The landscape
was here long before we were, it remains wild
when we do not. What sinters down is not love,
but longing, one life being never enough.
I have seen people frozen in attitudes
of loss, salted statues unchanged for years.

Dressing a Tree

I had to go back to the same yard
to find all had flown away,
strange air against me like a kiss.
There is only the tree now.
Finding it cannot leave, it throws out
blossoms, biting mimosa clouds.

Every time I visit I hang something on a branch.
A bell one time, a shell,
three bones,
a speckled feather tinged with blue.
The pomegranate was difficult to hang
and my soft brimmed hat turned like a penny.

Today, a photograph that shows you
just beginning to smile in that way you have, inviting.
This is my last dressing.
There is only the clack-clack of the shell and the bones.

Blossoms in the Wind

I thought it would change him
as grief does,
the turn away from chatter,

instead
to watch out of the window
where several geese string their way upriver.

Only recently Death crept to his neck,
licked a tender place, breathed softly
in the way that snow does.

Fear is the wolf.
Already he begins to forget,
He's alright now, he says, *alright.*

We must choose for ourselves.
See how the magnolia candles its flowers,
withstands the wind.

Doves in a Cherry Tree

You were talking of love,
singing your song of longing.

Over your shoulder I could see
two wood pigeons

sitting on the same branch
close to each other,

grey-feathered, white-ringed
closeness.

The cherry tree by the wall
held them on a branch –

wood pigeon pair sit close,
lapped by leaves.

Blackbird in the Night

It still felt like night,
the blackbird's first song around four,

his relaxed crooning up the garden
easing his family awake

and me too, open, clean, like a page,
lying in the shadowed room,

the dawn bird out on the cool tree.

Hearing Birds

First thing, like a fall of snowballs,
dawn raid of small feet to the roof,
starlings squeak and peck.
Wake to this untrodden time of birds,
bright air for swans to whirr by,
fan beat, necks stretch,
their full wings catch the light.

There is something about wild space,
how we fall to listening,
begin to hear birds' call,
wing-beat, lark-song.

We reach the headland to
shuffle into thick grass,
lie below a blued dome.
Here larks stitch song on song,
each carries silver threads higher,
small brown tailors,
up, over, notes pure tremor
until the sky field is alive.

Falling on my Feet

Crow swings on peanuts.
In the cold and bright,
he looks like a black flag.

The sun has come out,
a lemon light that happens
at this time of year.

I am falling on my feet,
coming to land, the hush of the breath,
all things written through with light.

Mis-timing

You brought in the body,
urgent in your misery,
wanting to honour.

I couldn't look at
the little dark body,
the feathers, the hooded shape.

You buried it somewhere.
I never saw.
I let you both down.

I want to say,
I'm sorry
about the wren.

One Thousand Birds
for Sadako Sasaki

In October, up to sixty thousand cranes
pass overhead, skeins of grey across the sky.
Here an installation of white paper cranes,
continuous rain from metal hooks,
birds dance through air, arc to the floor,
the smallest fade into the distance.

Wide windows throw sheets of light.
Sadako is in bed, aged twelve, folding her birds,
one thousand to ward off leukaemia.
She was almost two when the bomb flung her
from the breakfast table. Her family crouched all day
in a boat, in radioactive rain near Hiroshima.

Now she folds paper, this way, that way
to make a crane, folding to create the elongated neck,
the elegant sweep of wings. Sadako folds to make
a thousand birds for protection against her illness.
When she dies in October, her friends complete
the cranes, bury them with her.

Arctic Tern *(Sterna paradisaea)*

The terns are back,
I hear their sharp call *ki-ki,*
watch their quick hover, knife-dive.
They surge upward from the sea,
clean angled form.

I am quickened by the sight and sound
of these birds, thrill to their dive and recover.
They are beloved, Beloved.

In Silence

small waves break, dunlin
run the edge like leaves

it is early, a father tries to fly
a kite for his daughter

there is no wind, still he paces up
the beach, untangling string

a chain of grey geese clank across
blue space: there is silence inside

Woman Wading in Long Grass

There is wide blue lake,
there is mirrored water,
tuck tuck where the white egret watches.
All around the day falls, settles
its dusts, its wind currents.
It is as any other day,
the air has no date at all,
it could be any time.
Someone passes by in their car,
sun flashes on glass,
they see the birds pooled in light.

Just now, when I moved to the side,
I dislodged a frog. It jumped
and was gone like a thought,
perhaps I seemed like a dream.
So this is held in no frame,
this haze, this no particular moment.
Water ripples slightly,
reeds quiver,
there is sky above.

Walking and Light

We are not yet angels
walking, as we are, this bright field.
No matter where we go, our eyes seek light,
from wildest dazzle on water
to the duller gold of buttercup by a fence.

We found the River Lemon in winter,
walked along its banks. The water eased and rode around
islanded trees, made shallow pools. A rope swing hung in
    cold air,
cattle prints heft into mud by a gate. Above, a buzzard
    spirals its broad strength.
A shaft of sunlight showed us snowdrops on the bank,
    pure white.
A day of finding.

Then there is breath.
Slow to the breath.

Everything changes, we have only to be still and new
    aspects unfold.
The trees, for instance, how they shift and dance, lovely in
    their winter forms.
Even the land breathes, working with a slower time than
    ours.

Morning

I feel some catastrophe
is about to beset my teeth.
He strokes the top of my thigh,
while early morning light
polishes the end of the table.

The vari-coloured sweet peas
hold their heads up, graceful,
they seem to bounce with life,
the flower patch strung with
tendrilled reaching.

The cat has given up and settles.
What hidden hungers
make our need for touch?

Landscape

This morning I woke to
the smooth dune of your back
beloved land
body familiar.

Walk along a path
earth body
and
light
sea shine
glint of leaves
how snow makes shadows
with its thick cover
and your dear face
half-lit.

Landscape with rock
lovescape with hair
seascape with sail
and the long, smooth assembly
of your limbs on the bed.

The Wall

Everything I know
clamours inside,
shouts not to,

even so, here I am
leaning out a little
looking down.

Don't look down
he says, *look ahead.*
So I do

seeing a black roof,
sloped tiles,
the wide gap.

My heart decides
before I do.

Leaping

I was up there barefoot on the shiny bar,
high in the dust-spangled air,
where I could see the tops of heads,
the patterns the seats made.

I jumped, fell forward
into the thin air
with my eyes shut tight.

You caught me in warm arms,
so I began to breathe again.

I only live for this.

There was the feel of dancing,
a slow whirl
to when you brought me
to ground so gently
and left,
the air floated with promises and thrown kisses
already salt longing for the next time.
When I look up the trapeze is still swinging.

The Way Freedoms are Dreamt

I have purple hair in the dream,
purple hair, and I am standing
in full sun, tipping my head back.
This is familiar,
the way strange *is* familiar.

One of these crow-flecked days,
I will run fast down the road
right into the sea. Leave behind
the houses, with their pockets of dust,
their sleeping cats, the people with their
so-many different faces and needs.

No cupboards, no lists,
nothing to remember at all,
just the roar of it to absorb,
the echo and rumble that keep
larger time than a clock,
the wash that cleans to the bones.

Only the turn of waves, the spread
of spilt cream, the heave and arch,
getting ready to dive.

My Mother's Hand Mirror

My mother had a hand mirror, part of a set.
It was heavy in my childish grasp, backed
with impossibly blue, butterfly glass.

She was not glamorous, my mother,
though she made this gesture,
a stool where she never sat,
a mirror she never looked into,
but I was young, set to explore all things female.
I would tiptoe into her room, avoiding its adult smell
and my father's shoes, and lift the mirror.

The glass showed my eyes, quick green,
wild sticklebacks in a rain pond,
small teeth, toy piano keys,
red lips and cheeks, smudged by
the doll maker's impatient brush.

The mirror also showed future elephants,
the field of dreams we all go trumpeting to,
Alaska, over and over again,
a trapped princess in her tower –
what happened to her?

It showed lines of washing,
piles of gold and at a certain angle,
babies flew the walls.

Naming

Even now a wood has faint echoes.
The stars whistle words
that tell the trees their names.

So it is with a child. A life begins to form.
Everyone falls to listening. The mother tunes herself,
tries to hear a name.

When her baby is born, the stars call.
The stars do everything they can to be heard.
Some of us have corked ears,

we answer only to family voices.
Children struggle misnamed,
carry leaden coats for years.

Who has not sung in their bed at night,
found their true name, hugged its secret,
watched it flit away with the morning?

A Poem for Someone Who is Juggling Her Life

This is a poem for someone
who is juggling her life.
Be still sometimes.
Be still sometimes.

It needs repeating
over and over
to catch her attention
over and over,
as someone who is juggling her life
finds it difficult to hear.

Be still sometimes.
Be still sometimes.
Let it all fall sometimes.

Meditating on Cows

There are cows filling the road.
Black and white,
faltering past with their kind faces,
their ears that loop,
their great slack bodies, mud-splashed,
implacable as sideboards.

A face looms in the window,
wet-nosed, drips from one nostril.
Her eyes shine blackly, see and not see.
Her bulk knocks the wing mirror.
She startles into a run, sliding slightly,
uncomfortable just like my mother used to be
when she ran in slippered feet down the street.

Another is more curious, she stops to lick the door
and stares a second before others hurry her on.
They slop by, silent but for their feet,
dignity in their quiet obedience,
until the last walks by, flanked by the cowman,
who, relaxed and whistling, ties up the gate.

Smoke

If there is a perfect moment in the dream
when we arrive at the house we bought,
but keep forgetting about,
it is taking tea in the bath
and only eating almonds.
Then we sleep.

In my dream a naked woman cradles a seal.
I want so much to snatch it from her,
to throw it to the river, but feel shy,
so I light a cigarette. All abstemious years
fall away. I taste empty need again,
a curious comfort. It takes me back,
to stand outside and watch the sky at night,
the cobalt levels, the glowing tip,
blowing smoke to the stars.

I notice too, a toad leaning
on my foot. This is a good omen.

II

The Beaufort Scale and Points of the Year

When Looking for Birds

The walks are made in the first part of morning,
when bird activity is greatest.
The designated route is followed,
noting every bird seen or heard.

Care is taken so the same bird
is not counted more than once.
Time must be given when looking
for a particularly shy or hidden bird.

Survey work should not be carried out
in rain or winds above Beaufort four,
as birds will be in cover
and less likely to be vocal.

Found poem from an ornithologist's bird notes.

Heron

On the far edge of the estuary,
a flat oval that reflects light,
a heron is buffeted by strong winds.

He holds his ground, skinny legs planted,
points a determined beak into the force.
Feathers ruffled, he withstands,
the crest on his head in wild disarray.

March

Despite gale force winds
and heavy rain,
the cherry blossom is still
on its branches.

I Think About Death Every Day

When it is calm and smoke rises upward
like an illustration from a child's book,
even then, I sense the leaves rustle.
Weather vanes begin to move,
until litter slides along the road
and a plastic carrier bag dances in the air.

Her wooden coffin impenetrable,
I had to chant to myself over and over:
She's in there, she's in there
she is dead, she's in there.
I wished it were glass or at least
with a window for her face.

That brisk service,
the curtains and brick walls,
no place for an angel.
Outside we all shivered,
pretended to look at the wreaths,
while in the cellar they got on with
the business, fed her into the furnace
unwitnessed, for a fire-bright end.
Love cannot be assumed.

Later, her ashes were strangely heavy,
dry grey, sharp-edged, not soft
like the ashes from our hearth.
I hoped they would be white,
like Lux flakes, tiny panes of ivory
to fill my hand.

A Good Drying Day

Today, she prophesies,
the wind promises to rise.
Small trees in leaf begin to sway.
Eventually we usher out
the basket between us,
dead loaded with sodden sheets,
it creaks complaint.
Large branches buzz-saw air,
telegraph wires whistle warning cries.

We must be quick, before the increased swell
snatches our work from us.
Double the pegging, while the trees dance.
Wind wraps wet cloth around,
tugs sheet corners from hands.
Hare-eyed with effort, we fight
till fat sheets billow, crack and sail
over dull ground. Released,
I set off to where the woods
rock and smash on the hill.

My tree, with its easy climb, seats me
in canopy, where the whole wood
bucks and rolls, restless with waves.
Birds fix skinny legs, hang on
to ride out each buffeting shock
or take off, wheel wild, calling.
Twigs break off, whirl to the floor
with beech mast, old leaves, but I am high
in my crow's nest, wrapped in wood's roar,
quickened, while acres of clouds reel by.

The Storm

The sea churns,
so two young men must swim
to their boat tied way out,
bucking, like the metal horse
in our playground at home.

Fishermen tiptoe the edge,
try to haul fish life from it.

The early cormorants are long gone,
now three boys chuck stones,
as if to match the heave and thrust
of the very ocean we crawled from.

The wild sea excites, flags wave,
two couples huddle with hoods up,
shout to one another.
The young men have reached their boat.
Now what?

Mist blurs the headland,
soon the foghorn
will moan like a widow,
above the shapes lying deep in the bay.

Gale Force

On the table, a cup of wild flowers holds calm.
A gale warning has been issued,
up to seventy miles per hour, nine on the Beaufort Scale,
even so, it is wild already – hold on to
children and dogs, play lean-on-the-wind.

Waves foam white on to the rocks,
birds surf glanced air.
Like them we want to chance it, feel
the elemental surge, but we are puny,
soon return.

Out the window, pummelled dune-grass,
while the wind pushes at cabin walls,
which creak to become a ship.
Rock and roll,
we sail clean into the frothing sea.

Weather Warning

I try to raise it with him,
how he approaches love.
It's all about balance, I say,
right adjustment.

He doesn't understand.
Even the tulips he brought leap
from the vase, like snarling dragons.

He blows in at eight on the Beaufort Scale,
fresh gale, breaks twigs off trees,
impedes walking.

When he moves closer,
strong gale, slight damage to buildings,
chimney pots and slates blown off,
large branches down.

Within a month, it's gale force ten,
trees uprooted, widespread damage.
A weather warning. Get indoors.
Hurricane. Disastrous results.

Born

She is here –
she blew in at ten on the Beaufort Scale,
such a wild and windy night,
the rain lashed all day,
then gale force winds.
We had to drive around branches
lying broken in the road,
though where we found her
coddled at her mother's breast,
was calm
fathomed quiet.

A Year Turns

Cold morning through parted curtains,
another year opens, clear and fresh,
untrodden snow days.

Take down the calendar,
hang up a new one,
moon of completeness turns
to moon of beginning.
Time gifts another chance.

Those who watched the sky
for fireworks and bright stars,
weave their way home.

Out here, the day turns softly as a child in its sleep,
births quiet as the firstling lamb, which quivers
and shivers at its frosty delivery in a stall,
fragrant with iron and ice.

The fields lie silenced by winter,
fluffed birds seek food,
songless, with bright eyes.

Stoke up the fire, boil a kettle,
soon the kitchen will rattle
with welcome cooking.
Spill out the day, break eggs in the pan,
our first breakfast this year;
we are hungry.

Huccaby Hearth
St Raphael's Church, Huccaby, Dartmoor

Out here, February is as bad as it gets,
but this chapel, once a schoolhouse,
feels homely, with worn desks for pews
and stone fireplace, whose fire could kindle
children, their wet clothes and shoes.

I wish it was alight today,
though, I feel a warmth in this space,
hearth the more natural altar.
Outside, snowdrops drift the banks,
despite iced earth and the cutting wind.

My grandson is tucked in his village class,
dreaming of snow play. He woke excited,
his room snow-lit and strange,
while on the news they talk
of the terrible effects of snowfall.

Snow Trains

They send ghost trains to glide through the night,
but another presence wakes me early.
The snow really did fall at last,
clings to every twig and blade,
as blue light spreads over land.
Through quietened air, slow sun rises.

I walk out to a snow-viewing party,
bright litter of cones by the fir,
the creak of branches in dark tracery.
Coppiced willows, upright as tapers
at my grandmother's hearth.
A pheasant is in the snowfield,
soundless, he runs to the hedge,
a trail of brilliant colour.

Later, we creep home by snatched light
through snow, marbled on icy paths.
On Dartmoor, they listen for the ammil,
bent grasses spiral snow, every projecting thing
sheathed in ice. If the wind is gentle enough,
a chime will blow through icicles to charm the night.

In winter on Dartmoor a phenomenon occurs, known as the ammil, when ice
and frost coat everything, causing a musical sound as the wind blows.

Return

So cold, the frost
has feathered the window.

I am waiting for my daughter.
Through deep winter weeks
she has played down under,
swimming in warm pools.

Here the earth neglects itself,
in this quiet time, stone soil
is painted with ice.

Float an orange in a bowl
to tremble at her coming.
Prepare a table: apples for happiness,
honey for sweetness.
Write *Return* and burn it.

Drawn, she leaves the long dark,
but as she approaches my world,
first I hear a wave of birdsong
from newly leaved trees,
the chirp of goldcrest and sparrow.

We Stand in the Sun

This is the time of red,
a bunch of long stemmed roses.
We stand in the sun to remember
the soldiers who died.
A strong wind cracks at the flags,
Union Jack, Stars and Stripes.

A young naval officer speaks of how
the narrative of the Second World War
fired his childhood dreams.
He talks in his gentle, film star voice
of *the fog of war*, own goals in the theatre of war.
Behind them all, the black tank, like Death,
the floral dress of the mayoress.

On the First Day of Autumn

The air anticipates change, sudden heavy rain,
monsoon drops as big as stones. The shift begins,
blackbirds feed on rowan berries, cattle eat wet grass.
We feel the chill, begin to wear coats,
clouds part to let colder sun through, then close.
The flick of a light switch.

We live under the flight path of the greylag geese,
whose V grows longer each day. With the house martins gone,
apples litter the grass, the sumac hangs its prayer flags for
    gilding.
We join a lantern walk at night,
note the full moon over us, await season's turn,
taste dry wind and death, hide bulbs in the ground.

Make tracks for the feast of ingathering, plenty for a mouse,
plenty for a hen: seed pods, pinecones, fruit and feast.
Hold up an ear of corn. Listen, what's coming toward us?
Open a pomegranate the right way, quarter-wise,
my mother showed me. Part gently for rubies we eat from
    a pin.
We have sown, we have tended, grown up and gathered.

Bless Corn Mother, present and absent.
Bless this company here at the feast.
Bless the fire, the waters, the earth.
Bless the birds that fly home to roost.
Bless breath, inquisitive air.
Bless life, joyfully lived.

III

The Other Leaves on the Tree

Casting Off

She should have let him go ages before
he asked her, several times, I heard him,
but she stood thigh deep, her small hands on
the prow of his boat, offering instructions
in a gentle voice, as an air hostess does before
take off, her own fears chained together
like clauses and carefully wrapped around
as fast as he tries to cast off, until he can
take it no more and shouts to her to let go
and to shut up, since he knows more about sailing
than she does, so she stands with her arms
at her sides, watching, while the wind takes
her son and his orange sails and carries him out
far on a run, so he cuts through the slate sea
not looking back, but we can just hear his voice:
I know far more about sailing than you do.

On Bringing Up Girls

Aren't you going to clip her wings?
they said, *That's usual for a girl her age, isn't it?*
We said we didn't want to clip her wings
and they watched our little daughter grow
bright and strong, then they said

Aren't you going to tie her feet? That's
advisable for a young girl, isn't it?
We said we didn't want to tie her feet,
so they saw a young woman growing
clear and brave. Before they could say anything else
we said, *Now it is time to teach her to fly.*
They fell back.

They are teaching her to fly, they repeated,
teaching her to fly.
How wonderful, murmured their daughters,
and how interesting.

Take Them Back

Sometimes I look down and there is Marilyn Monroe
    standing in my shoes,
my body feels gorgeous in my gaga dress.
She blows red kisses before her candle goes out
and I wonder who could ever not love this woman.

Sometimes I look down and there is a little girl standing
    in my shoes.
All she does is cry, so her raven shoes are sodden with
    tears
and have white salt lines, which never come off, no matter
    how often
you polish them. She wonders why no one loves her.

Sometimes I look down and there is my mother standing
    in my shoes,
which are comfortable and worn. Her feet are so tired.
She has walked a long way and I wonder,
how do I love this woman who is no longer here?

Sometimes I look down and find pointy black high-heeled
    boots on my feet,
but they are not mine at all. Perhaps they are yours?
Please take them back.
I can never love these shoes.

Sometimes I look down and my feet disappear
and then, most of all then, I wonder who could possibly
    love this woman,
she does not even know who she is.

Who could possibly love this aching woman
over here – no, over here – who is trying to find a place to
    stand,
who hangs on to hope like a ragged tune,
who has caught a kiss from Marilyn Monroe?

Second Time

The second time I met you it was your lunch hour
and you were walking up the street
as if you had clown's boots on
and I said, *Why are you walking like a clown?*
And you freaked out and said you weren't,
you were walking normally, but with awareness
and you stomped off, carefully,
still wearing your boots
and I remember thinking how funny you were
and that your hair shone blue in the sun.

Tilt

Sugar   frame   halo   light
right there in the doorway
like a snapshot, like it's all a dream
and we haven't really grown old
like we had it all to discover

you always look young like that
not wearing coats, not carrying bags
not minding the rain, that straight look
unnerving so I answer too quickly
tumbling it all out more than I mean to

watching your hand slide over where
your knee makes a bridge and the sun
shines the air up, filled with dust motes
sugar and all time stops
like a photograph
                    smile

Singing Lessons

For almost a year now
I have marked my notebook with a card,
which offers me lessons in
The Art of Mongolian Overtone Singing.

It started as a joke, this little card,
the strange thing is, due to daily exposure,
I now think of *The Art of Mongolian
Overtone Singing* as commonplace, with
its beguiling images of white yurts against blue sky
and wide yellow plain with figures on horseback.

I consider whether my life needs
The Art of Mongolian Overtone Singing,
perhaps it is precisely these harmonics
that it lacks.

I think of my father singing fragments of *Carmen*
in the bathroom. My mother would whisper
that he had the best bass voice in his school.
He put us all in the church choir, where we learnt
hymns and how to eat fruit gums undetected.

I may never escape the tribe of Baby Boomers
into which I was born, continually seeking outside
our culture, to find satisfaction or overtone singing,
but, I wonder what Mongolians long for.

Breaking

The summer my boy broke himself
something broke in me,
as if my wings had been snatched off,
my antennae bent,
so I could not feel ahead
and everything turned dull grey.
There was no healing at all.

People turned away their ears,
their eyes, their faced hearts,
as if breaking is contagious
and that breaking is the worst thing you can do.

Love May Visit

If I should deserve it,
bring me your fierce love,
like the dragonfly that pushed its way
into my kitchen that day and filled
the whole room with its buzzing
and need to breed, fluttering at
the paper dragonfly in the fern
till I lifted it up on my finger
and carried it to the outside air,
with its magnificent wings
and its striped angry head
and its muscled legs which trembled
and clung light and trusting to my skin,
then flew straight up like
an aquamarine helicopter thief.

Don't Go

Let's not talk about loss.
Let's instead mention oranges,
bright in a blue bowl
or remember snow,
how it crunches, how it seeps cold
into the finger bones.

Let us talk, not of the end,
but of tulips, rain.

It's dreadful getting old.
You forget your three hats,
your beautiful shoes,
most of the lovers
whose skin you've smoothed.
You don't forget the love somehow.

There was a cast-iron gate,
heavy to push, it groaned
like the giant Sisyphus.
Someone said we must try
to imagine Sisyphus happy.
We try to be happy.

Don't go. Tonight there'll be stars.
It's a clear night, a sickle moon.
That's my cat scratching,
she is my grandmother come back.
I try not to give her a hard time.
She bites.

Two Cups

Now she's dead I do it all the time.
I'm always setting out two cups for tea.
I bought her favourite biscuits just last week,
I can't get used to not having her here.
There's no one else to tell about the birds
or when *The Archers* start or to ask
if we should risk the plants out overnight.
The frost might come and then you've lost the lot.
I'm always setting out two cups for tea
and shouting her it's raining, but she's gone.
A woman comes to clean. She's very nice.
She doesn't talk much though and we don't laugh.
I find I have too much time by myself.
I'd give anything to have her back again.

Greenhouse

Show me a greenhouse,
I catch my grandad's face,
turning as he bends to his plants,
his calm back rounded away
from trench war and toil.
I recall his gentleness,
the pungent hothouse smell
of tomato plants and the soil,
quick with growing.

A swallow chatters above
the greenhouse door.
Close, the soft bloom of its breast,
the dark pointed wings folded.

One of the greenhouses holds
sweet peas, growing up
on rows of wigwam sticks,
and roses, crowds of deep faces,
blowsy and soft,
the atmosphere heavy, sweet.

Dry earth, glasshouse,
warm air pouring around,
a room full of quiet,
so I want to lie down among the stalks
to watch the light make its way
through petals.

On Setting Out To Find the Way Back

In winter, start from your own back door,
walk a long, cobbled street, then
face north, up the hill to the park
to a blackened stone gateway.
Cross a bridge, past bushes, the shelter,
dodge several fierce swans who hiss by the lake,
pick up lost leaves, you will need them for later,
visit the sundial set in the east.

Now, take the path to pace round the fountain,
step on the iced circle, if you still dare,
wish your best wish, throw in a coin,
send it, and the wish, skittering there.
Make for the bandstand set on the slope,
unearth an old dream a child left there.
Sing your heart out.

Follow the path round the west of the park,
past the greenhouse with neat plants in rows,
head up the steps which lead to the terrace.
Stand by each statue, renew their acquaintance:
Apollo, Hercules, Athena, Diana.
Along to the summer house, once painted yellow,
at the back, on the bench, there it is,
pick it up.

Sean O'Casey's Pond

The train is late;
heat tricks along the lines.
We sit resigned.
We are British and this our rail,
our station, which received
one bomb during the war,
its casualty, a man sitting
in the waiting room.
A direct hit.

Our station, with its white picket fence,
its chiming bells and apologies,
a pigeon coddling her brood
in the rafters and the lily pond
on platform two, placed there by
Sean O'Casey during his sojourn
in Totnes, and happy chance that
he did, the pond with its goldfish
and several lily flowers and its
water boatmen is a small eye
to borrowed heaven, reflecting
the sky, the hovering damselfly
and our peering faces.

In Love and Aviation

And so as we take off,
the cheerful man in the seat next to me,
with his giant RAF watch
with gold wings for hands
and his crowned winged badge in his lapel
and his blazer with brass buttons,
asks me if I understand the principles of flight.

He takes out his pen
and draws a diagram on his newspaper,
explaining in a friendly voice about wing shape,
drag and lift, and airflow.
It is all a question of balance.

I understand.
It is the same impossibility with love.
Later, I point out the light auras on the propellers,
how they look like cartoon drawings.

Ah yes, he says, *the haloes,*
and he smiles.

A Close Call

The skinny, angelic girl told me
she saw a bear come out
of its cave in Bavaria

one frosty morning
when the sky was egg-blue,
but the air dazzled with white

and although she made the mistake
of introducing the bear to Damien Hirst,
who talked excitedly on his mobile,

it dealt with the matter quickly
by ripping his heart out
with a sharp pointed bear nail.

Caged

You remember my uncle?
He was caged for months with
a Bavarian bear. He fed it apples
and the greater share of his food.

One night, he woke to find the bear staring
into his face, its muzzle inches from his throat.
It kissed him on the forehead.
Its breath smelt of red berries and snow.

He fell into a dream in which
he was dancing with a swan,
which was wife to him,
that is they moved as one.

They nested on an island in a lake.
On their wedding day
there were fires and music,
all the time in the world.

Returning from his dream, my uncle woke
to find the bear outside the cage
in an attitude of guardianship.
The door had gone.

Buffalo

I went to the zoo and sat by a fence,
right near the head of a sleeping buffalo,
I sat there for a long time while he slept.

His head was massive, warm and heavy.
He shuffled a little in his sleep.
I sat by him until I was still as a prairie and wide.

He showed me some mystery and wildness
and that he still had his dreams.

On Never Asking Questions and a Happy Ending

We never used to ask questions about Wednesdays,
they came and went, without our knowing why.
One Wednesday, though, my grandad came to call,
he popped in and didn't go away.
We put him in the box room with a wardrobe.
There was just space for his slippers and a bed.
He said that was plenty to be going on with,
that soon he'd take up even less, so there.

We all got used to Grandad's little habits,
like how he stirred his tea a hundred times,
creating mini whirlpools in his teacups
and how he'd cry sometimes, sigh loudly,
or just stare. Then he would insist we all play
dominoes or the piano or hunt the thimble or just cards.
We didn't mind, he was no trouble, he was Grandad.

One day, though, a Wednesday as it happens,
I came home from school to find him gone.
He'd eloped with somebody called Beryl,
a cocktail waitress from Burnley he knew well.
After that, we just saw him at Christmas
wearing cowboy boots, gold lamé shirt and tie.
He said he'd never been so happy
and thanked us for minding him that spell.

My Brother's Gift

He gave it suddenly, carefully,
wrapped in black tissue. A strange surprise,
hard and bevelled, the colour of sand.

It smelt dry, a fetal thing, frozen curiosity
made by itself, a marvel from underneath,
quiet, secret growth which accretes,

as trust does, amounting to something
almost beautiful. A desert rose,
treasure formed out of sight,

bloomed in barren conditions,
sand coral, formed far from any sea.
That is his quiet way.

The Seagull and the Biker

World Cup night police car parked
on quay ready for trouble
inside they look edgy hot edgy
in short haircuts short sleeved shirts
blue edgy blue edgy
jam sandwich in the sun wilco

Sunny evening Captain Jasper's
sugar spoon winks on hot chain
hot but next to us this guy
squeezed into bike leathers
red leather Super Harley hero

Seagull flies by no surprise this seagull city
smell fish everywhere
fishing boats harbour oil slicked water
chip fish wrappers over black water
this seagull though this different seagull
holds ten pound note in mouth yes
it opens beak to cry out seagull call
note flutters falls small flutter rests
lightly on green petrol not-Mediterranean
sea surface right near Super Harley hero man

Can't believe his eyes stare bend
leather cracks adjust sunglasses against glare
hey girlfriend over here she's tidy slim
flower dress laughs lift me in lift me down
mermaid dip toes-tail blond hair falls
muscled he holds her over black treacle
catch fish note with webbed toes catch
he hauls her in swings her up
together they spread prize dry hot table
look into smile laugh kiss

Lighthouse Keeper

He smells of oil and Windolene
and is about to be made redundant
by automation. He shows us
the model ship he made from used matches.
His tower-base room is browned gloss paint and pipes.
Green stairs pile above us now,
curving up and up
like hopes, like smoke,
like whispers creeping thinner.

He is eager to connect,
the way he offers tea,
the way he floods the saucers.
He is sorry there are no biscuits,
but we can see the Light Room.
It isn't on now, of course,
just prismed glass layered like hard roses,
polished ready for the stone-lonely turning of the night.

In the old days they used candles,
but now the generator sees to it.
There is enough power to light a ballroom.
He is going to miss sitting up here of a night,
working shifts to make sure all is ship-shape,
the wild sounding of the wind,
the gearing clicks, the sea always at a roar,
the harassed rocks, the metal tick of the timer.
Mostly he'll miss the stars.

A Hearth Maid in Elizabeth's Court

I have to set the fires of a morning,
usually I'm the first one up,
though several times I have come across her,
walking the corridors at dawn or sitting
before an empty grate. No candles.
She has a fixity about her face at those times,
as if it is carved from stone,
though her eyes blaze.
She is one for deep thought,
they say she never confides.

I think she doesn't notice me,
I tiptoe about my business.
I'll tell you this, she feels sad
and lonely as a tower.
I have seen tears shine on her cheeks
and once, in cloaked dark, a man lay at her feet.

What is a Cathedral?

It is a place of air and thrown light,
so many windows you can maze yourself.
It's still, great pillars stand like redwoods,
dwarf us, so we look like children in the woods.
It has a font, of course, for baby blessing,
and bells, for calling.

A cathedral says: look up, look right up,
wander with your eyes upturned,
again like children,
see fruit-gummed glass,
feel ancient stone under your feet,
find angels, angels everywhere.

It has carved corpses, frozen as in death,
an organ, whose pipes form a sleeping face,
the largest ones like foghorns on big ships,
old threadbare flags, that hang in quiet rows
and empty pews.
It has a shop, souvenirs, no loos.

Behind the choir stall is the Bishop's throne,
his mitred chair a triumph of dark shapes.
Even so, it is the roof that takes me high,
the flutes and fans of vaulted ribs
that tell the heart to fly.
It is the inside of Jonah's whale.

Bellever Blues

The youth hostel frightens and annoys
a part of me that refuses the notices, plastic flowers,
the neglected dragon plant by the sink.

It does not feel young at all,
the wildlife posters blued by the sun.
Outside a horse laughs.

In Case of Emergency Throw Lifebelt

In case of lifebelt, shout *help*.
In case of help, show gratitude.
In case of gratitude, open heart.
In case of openness, see what is.
In case of what is, know life.
In case of life, love people.
In case of people, have humour.
In case of humour, be kind.
In case of kindness, pay forward.
In case of paying forward, be generous.
In case of generosity, spread freely.
In case of freedom, fly far.
In case of flying far, watch for destiny.
In case of destiny, expect emergencies.
In case of emergencies, throw lifebelt.

Rules For Poet Hurling

1. If a poet is thrown through a glass window or glass door, he must wear gloves and a suitable mask.

2. If a poet is thrown through a burning hoop, extinguishers must be provided.

3. If a poet is thrown down a well, the organisers must ensure that the bottom of the well is dry, and is covered by leaves to a depth of three inches.

4. If a poet is to be thrown across the path of an oncoming train, the thrower must previously satisfy the organisers that he bears no personal malice to the throwee.

5. If a poet is thrown into a pond or river, he must wear a wetsuit and need not be tightly bound.

6. If poets are thrown at night, they may be painted with phosphorescent paint, so that the point of impact may be clearly established.

7. If a poet refuses to be bound in the usual way before throwing, he may be put in a straitjacket of the requisite size. If no straitjacket is available, two or three brassieres may be used.

8. If a poet utters any sound whatsoever, either in flight or at the moment of impact, the throw will be disqualified.

9. If a disc jockey impersonates a poet, and wins a competition because his light weight allows him to be thrown farthest, he will be liable to a fine of £1000 or three years' imprisonment.

10. It is strictly forbidden in poet hurling literature and publicity to refer to poets as 'short writers' or 'persons of restricted writing'.

Adapted from a poem by Edwin Morgan.

You Don't Need to Wear a Fish Head to Feel Weird

Now my skin colours itself,
like that on rice pudding,
I get this nutmeg feeling,
turn my unnecessary attention
to a rust patch on the wall.

I stay up all night, drink
till I throw up. Whatever.
No one minds. At least my eyes
aren't too small to see, at least
I know I'm not a swan.

I know what's happening:
transversal disintegration. Yeah.
I've done this before, but then
it was cool. Just get in the swing.
Before you know it, you're humming.

This time it's like light chains
looped right round. No sweat.
Identities crack through
to other stuff always there.
You don't have to see straight all the time.

No need to worry, honey.
What slips away was never meant
to stay. Honey.
Notice my eyelash still curves,
doing what it should.

Big Questions

Does God have a face
and why are we here?
What is the answer?
How would we know?

Why do you look so lost
leaning your arms on the table
waiting for your tea to cool?

Is anyone found?
Is there an always?
Can people really die of never?

Who began all this?
Who makes the rules?
What closes hearts?
How can we learn to love?

Is kindness genetic?
Have you ever seen a kingfisher?
Does anything matter?
How long do I have?

Why do you shake your head
and watch me with sad eyes?
Don't you hear it?
Don't you feel it in your feet?

Tumble it all down,
to the whispering beeches
to the brown birds
which sing up the night.

Big Answers

Never trust a man with green eyes.
Never mind the gap.
Never look in the cupboard in the attic.
Never act as if you know.

Never forget to wash your hands.
Never underestimate kindness.
Never love aimlessly and low.

Never touch me there.
Never did.
Never land.

Never ever do that again.
Never touch my hair.
Always behave as if you mean it.
Live with only a few weeks left.

Never lose that longing.
Never doubt.
Never believe you were a mistake.
Never let go and remember that

never having heard the whisper of stars
does not mean that
you cannot dance
at the imagining of it.

Here it is,
here, quivering in your breath
waiting for you
to belong.

Acknowledgements

Some of these poems have appeared in the following poetry magazines: *The Shop, Smiths Knoll, Raindog, Envoi, Popularity Contest, Magma, Flying Post, Obsessed With Pipework, Anemone Sidecar, Artemis, Tiferet, Damselfly Press, Symmetry Pebbles, Ink, Turbulence* and *The Bakery,* and in various publications: *Poetry On the Buses* edited by Valerie Belsey and Candy Neubert (Green Books 2001); *In Love* (Leaf Books 2006); *Hidden Histories* edited by Greta Stoddart (University of Exeter 2008); *Everyday Festival* by Rose Cook (Happen*Stance* Press 2009); *Seductive Harmonies: The Poetry of Music* edited by Deborah Gaye (Avalanche Books 2011); and *Running Before the Wind* edited by Joy Howard (Greyhen Press 2013).

Special thanks to all those who offered feedback and support during the writing of this collection.

Cultured Llama Publishing

hungry for poetry
thirsty for fiction

Cultured Llama was born in a converted stable. This creature of humble birth drank greedily from the creative source of the poets, writers, artists and musicians that visited, and soon the llama fulfilled the destiny of its given name.

Cultured Llama is a publishing house, a multi-arts events promoter and a fundraiser for charity. It aspires to quality from the first creative thought through to the finished product.

www.culturedllama.co.uk

Also published by Cultured Llama

A Radiance
by Bethany W. Pope

Paperback; 70pp; 203x127mm;
978-0-9568921-3-3; June 2012
Cultured Llama

Family stories and extraordinary images glow throughout this compelling debut collection from an award-winning author, like the disc of uranium buried in her grandfather's backyard. *A Radiance* 'gives glimpses into a world both contemporary and deeply attuned to history – the embattled history of a family, but also of the American South where the author grew up.'

> 'A stunning debut collection ... these poems invite us to reinvent loss as a new kind of dwelling, where the infinitesimal becomes as luminous as ever.'
>
> Menna Elfyn

'*A Radiance* weaves the voices of four generations into a rich story of family betrayal and survival, shame and grace, the visceral and sublime. A sense of offbeat wonder at everyday miracles of survival and love both fires these poems and haunts them – in a good way.'

Tiffany S. Atkinson

'An exhilarating and exceptional new voice in poetry.'

Matthew Francis

Also published by Cultured Llama

strange fruits
by Maria C. McCarthy

Paperback; 72pp; 203x127mm;
978-0-9568921-0-2; July 2011
Cultured Llama (in association with
WordAid.org.uk)

Maria is a poet of remarkable skill, whose work offers surprising glimpses into our 21st-century lives – the 'strange fruits' of our civilisation or lack of it. Shot through with meditations on the past and her heritage as 'an Irish girl, an English woman', *strange fruits* includes poems reflecting on her urban life in a Medway town and as a rural resident in Swale.

Maria writes, and occasionally teaches creative writing, in a shed at the end of her garden.

All profits from the sale of *strange fruits* go to Macmillan Cancer Support, Registered Charity Number 261017.

'Maria McCarthy writes of the poetry process: "There is a quickening early in the day" ('Raising Poems'). A quickening is certainly apparent in these humane poems, which are both natural and skilful, and combine the earthiness and mysteriousness of life. I read *strange fruits* with pleasure, surprise and a sense of recognition.'

Moniza Alvi

Canterbury Tales on a Cockcrow Morning
by Maggie Harris

Paperback; 136pp; 203x127mm;
978-0-9568921-6-4; September 2012
Cultured Llama

Maggie Harris brings warmth and humour to her *Canterbury Tales on a Cockcrow Morning* and tops them with a twist of calypso.

Here are pilgrims old and new: Eliot living in 'This Mother Country' for half a century; Samantha learning that country life is not like in the magazines.

There are stories of regret, longing and wanting to belong; a sense of place and displacement resonates throughout.

> 'Finely tuned to dialogue and shifting registers of speech, Maggie Harris' fast-moving prose is as prismatic as the multi-layered world she evokes. Her Canterbury Tales, sharply observed, are rich with migrant collisions and collusions.'

John Agard

The Strangest Thankyou
by Richard Thomas

Paperback; 98pp; 203x127mm;
978-0-9568921-5-7; October 2012
Cultured Llama

Richard Thomas's debut poetry collection embraces the magical and the mundane, the exotic and the everyday, the surreal rooted in reality.

Grand poetic themes of love, death and great lives are cut with surprising twists and playful use of language, shape, form and imagery.

The poet seeks 'an array of wonder' in "Dig" and spreads his 'riches' throughout *The Strangest Thankyou*.

> 'He has long been one to watch, and with this strong, diverse collection Richard Thomas is now one to read. And re-read.'

Matt Harvey

Unauthorised Person
by Philip Kane

Paperback; 74pp; 203x127mm;
978-0-9568921-4-0; November 2012
Cultured Llama

Philip Kane describes *Unauthorised Person* as a 'concept album' of individual poems, sequences, and visuals, threaded together by the central motif of the River Medway.

This collection draws together poems written and images collected over 27 years, exploring the psychogeography of the people and urban landscapes of the Medway Towns, where 'chatham high street is paradise enough' ("johnnie writes a quatrain").

> 'This collection shows a poet whose work has grown in stature to become strong, honest and mature. Yet another voice has emerged from the Medway region that I'm sure will be heard beyond our borders. The pieces here vary in tone, often lyrical, sometimes prosaic but all show a deep rooted humanity and a political (with a small p) sensibility.'

Bill Lewis

Also published by Cultured Llama

Unexplored Territory
edited by Maria C. McCarthy

Paperback; 112pp; 203x127mm;
978-0-9568921-7-1; November 2012
Cultured Llama

Unexplored Territory is the first anthology from Cultured Llama – poetry and fiction that take a slantwise look at worlds, both real and imagined.

'A dynamic range of new work by both established and emerging writers, this anthology offers numerous delights.

The themes and preoccupations are wide-ranging. Rooted in close observation, the poems and short fiction concern the 'unexplored territory' of person and place.

A must for anyone who likes good writing.'

Nancy Gaffield
author of *Tokaido Road*

Contributors:

Jenny Cross
Maggie Drury
June English
Maggie Harris
Mark Holihan
Sarah Jenkin

Philip Kane
Luigi Marchini
Maria C. McCarthy
Rosemary McLeish
Gillian Moyes
Bethany W. Pope

Hilda Sheehan
Fiona Sinclair
Jane Stemp
Richard Thomas
Vicky Wilson

Also published by Cultured Llama

The Night My Sister
Went to Hollywood
by Hilda Sheehan

Paperback; 82pp; 203x127mm;
978-0-9568921-8-8; March 2013
Cultured Llama

In *The Night My Sister Went To Hollywood* Hilda
Sheehan offers poems on love, exhaustion, classic movies, supermarket
shopping and seals in the bathtub. Her poems 'bristle with the stuff of
life'. Her language is 'vigorous and seductively surreal'. 'What kind of
a mother writes poems / anyway, and why?' she asks. A mother of five,
Hilda Sheehan is that kind of mother. Read this debut poetry collection
now: 'time is running out … Asda will shut soon'.

> I was constantly impressed by a sense of voice, and a wonderful
> voice, clear and absolutely achieved. Throughout … domestic
> imagery makes of the kitchen and the household tasks a
> contemporary epic. The deceptively trivial detail of our daily
> lives works just as in Dickens, a great collector of trivia, and
> the pre-Raphaelites, revealing a powerful gift for metaphor. As
> Coleridge said, metaphor is an important gift of the true poet,
> and Hilda Sheehan has that gift in abundance.
>
> William Bedford
> author of *Collecting Bottle Tops: Selected Poetry 1960-2008*

> It's one thing to have a vivid imagination. It's another to be adept
> at language. It's quite another to be gifted with the language
> to release and express that imagination. Hilda Sheehan has all
> three. She has the ability to see the pathos – as well as the joie
> de vivre – in the human comedy, and to convey it in a vigorous
> and sometimes seductively surreal language. We are enabled to
> see what we may not have been able or prepared to see, or even
> thought of seeing: this is what poetry is all about.
>
> Robert Vas Dias
> author of *Still-Life and Other Poems of Art and Artifice*

Lightning Source UK Ltd.
Milton Keynes UK
UKOW04f1301040214

225842UK00001B/6/P